300 Incredib
Things to Do
on the Internet

VIP Publishing
Marietta, Georgia • (800) 909-6505
Distributed by M.K. Distributors, Inc.

ISBN 0-9658668-0-7

About the Author

Ken Leebow has been in the computer business for over 20 years. The Internet has fascinated him since he began exploring its riches a few years ago, and he has helped thousands of individuals and businesses understand and utilize its resources.

When not on the Net, you can find Ken playing tennis, running, reading or spending time with his family. He is living proof that being addicted to the Net doesn't mean giving up on the other pleasures of life.

Introduction

Many people believe the Internet will dramatically change all of our business and personal lives. Ultimately, this may be true. However, the explanation I like best is that it is "fun and useful."

As illustrated on the cover of this book, the Internet spans an unlimited array of subjects. Randomness rules, and every click of the mouse can instantly propel you to another data universe.

Use this book as a guide to surf the Net, have fun and find some useful information for yourself.

Ken Leebow
Leebow@News-letter.com
http://this.is/TheLeebowLetter

P.S. Many thanks to Paul Joffe and Janet Bolton, of TBI Creative Services, for design and editing help.

1
The Leebow Letter

http://this.is/TheLeebowLetter

This is my site. It has information about our company and literally thousands of other sites (organized by category) for you to visit.

2
PointCast

http://www.pointcast.com

This is a valuable news and information source with excellent graphics.

3
RealAudio

http://www.realaudio.com

Listen to all the fantastic educational information provided by this audio technology. If you get tired of education, you can listen to the Grateful Dead 24 hours a day.

4
Infobeat

http://www.infobeat.com

You name it, and Infobeat will e-mail it to you: sports, news, weather, Internet information, stocks and more. Push (delivery) technology is the way to go, and Infobeat leads the pack in this area.

5
What Does That Automobile Cost?

http://www.edmunds.com

http://www.kbb.com

http://msn.carpoint.com

Finally, you can be on equal footing with car dealers. No doubt, you will know more about new cars than the salesperson.

6
Portfolio Tracking

http://investor.msn.com

http://quote.yahoo.com

If you want to track your stocks, Yahoo! and Microsoft will be happy to assist you.

7
Excited About Lycos

http://www.excite.com
http://www.lycos.com
Two excellent search engines on the Net. Excite and Lycos provide maps, an e-mail search and a lot more.

8
Juno

http://www.juno.com
Juno has software that will allow you to send e-mail for free. If your friends and family don't have e-mail, give them this free gift.

9
Wall Street Journal

http://www.wsj.com
One of the best print publications on the Net.

10
Pathfinder (Time/Warner)

http://pathfinder.com

Money, People, Fortune, Time, Sports Illustrated and more. This is one of the best places on the Net to visit. You can even subscribe to a weekly e-mail reminder.

11
PRARS

http://www.prars.com

Want an annual report on any one of 3,200 corporations? This is your site.

12
Trip.com

http://www.thetrip.com

Track airline flights and view hotel, restaurant and weather information for particular cities.

13
Look Smart

http://www.looksmart.com

Yes, you will look smart after visiting here. You name it, and this place has the information.

14
Census Data

http://govinfo.kerr.orst.edu

Simply and easily, get census data about any area in the U.S. Just put in the zip code.

15
Hot Wired and the World

http://www.hotwired.com/rough

If you want information on a city in Mexico, Europe, Canada, Australia, India, Hong Kong or the USA, check this site out. Hot Wired helps you find out about lodging, dining and entertainment.

16
National Debt

http://www.toptips.com/debtclock.html
Keep track of how deep in hock Uncle Sam is.

17
Movies

http://us.imdb.com
Everything you ever needed to know about movies. This is the ultimate movie site on the Net.

18
Wanna Buy a Book?

http://www.amazon.com
http://www.barnesandnoble.com
If you want to buy books, these are two great sites on the Net. There are reviews, interviews and more waiting for you. Of course, you can easily search for a book.

19
Gutenberg Project

http://www.promo.net/pg

If a book is in the public domain, it is probably located (in its entirety) at the Gutenberg Project.

20
Take Me to Your Leader

http://www.trytel.com/~aberdeen

http://www.geocities.com/Athens/1058/rulers.html

Who runs the countries of the world? Find out here. You can also obtain mailing addresses and Web sites.

21
Ticketmaster

http://www.ticketmaster.com

Go here if you need tickets or a seating chart for just about any event.

22
Auto Lease vs. Purchase

http://leasesource.com

http://www.search.com/Single/0%2C7%2C400503%2C00.html

Learn about car leasing and do calculations here before negotiating a lease.

23
Auto-By-Tel

http://www.autobytel.com

Yes, you can buy a car on the Net. Auto-By-Tel even promises that you will get a great deal.

24
Inaugural Speeches

http://www.columbia.edu/acis/bartleby/inaugural

From George Washington to Bill Clinton, they're all here.

25
Political Junkies

http://www.allpolitics.com

If you love politics, you shouldn't miss this site.

26
Compare Political Views

http://voter96.cqalert.com/cq_rate.htm

Compare your views with your congressman's.

27
Medical Information

http://www.mwsearch.com

Need some medical information? Check out this excellent search engine.

28
E-mail to Fax

http://www.faxsav.com

http://www.faxaway.com

Learn how to send e-mail to someone's fax machine. You can send it anywhere in the world, and it's free.

29
Internet Public Library

http://www.ipl.org

If you can't find a good piece of information here, you are not a living, breathing human being.

30
Birthday Calendar

http://www.eb.com/calendar/cal2.htm

http://www.eb.com/calendar/calendar.html

Plan ahead. This calendar lists the birthdays of some well-known personalities.

31
Newspapers Everywhere

http://newo.com/news

http://www.newslink.org

http://www.voyager.co.nz/~vag118/news.html

http://www.all-links.com/newscentral

There are tons of great newspapers on the Net. You will certainly be able to find all of them here.

32
Resources Galore

http://www.beaucoup.com/engbig.html

Looking for something on the Net? This is a good page to use to find almost anything.

33

Financial Information on the Net

http://www.streeteye.com
http://www.bigcharts.com
http://www.dailystocks.com
http://www.stockscreener.com
http://www.dbc.com
http://www.doh.com

The Net and stocks go together. These sites will keep you so informed and up to date that your broker will be calling you for advice.

34

Forbes 400

http://www.forbes.com/tool/toolbox/rich97/index.asp

Check out a list of the richest people in America.

35
Four Legends

http://www.unitedmedia.com/comics/dilbert
http://www.marthastewart.com
http://www.elvispresley.com
http://www.sinatra.com

Dilbert, Martha, Elvis and Frank…they have not left the Net.

36
Trade Shows

http://www.tscentral.com

Need a good excuse to get out of town? Check out this site to see where there is a good trade show. It has them for just about any industry and in many countries. Happy learning, partying and traveling.

37
Mutual Funds

http://www.mfea.com
http://www.morningstar.net
http://www.worth.com
On the Net, these are your guides to mutual funds.

38
I'm a Newbie

http://www.pbs.org/uti/begin.html
PBS provides great information for newbies (those who are new to the Net).

39
Dictionaries

http://www.onelook.com
This site has over 50 dictionaries in various topics such as: technology, telephony, religion, business terms and more.

40
Take the Test

http://www.davideck.com

Want to know your IQ? How about your personality? Go to this site for a lot of tests.

41
Historical Weather

http://www.weatherpost.com/historical/historical.htm

This database offers a huge amount of weather details for over 2,000 cities.

42
Living In The Past

http://www.retroactive.com

Ah, the good old days. If you want to go back a few years in time, here is the place to do it.

43
Purchase One Share of Stock

http://www.oneshare.com

This is not intended to be your place to trade stocks on the Internet. Its purpose is for gift items. For example, the hottest sellers are Apple Computer and the Boston Celtics.

44
Merriam Webster Dictionary

http://www.m-w.com/dictionary

Yep, Mr. Webster's dictionary is on the Net. It even has a "word for the day" section.

45
The Washington Post

http://www.washingtonpost.com

Straight from the Nation's Capital.

46
The Next Millennium

http://www.year2000.com

Trouble is waiting for us in the year 2000. Read all about it.

47
AMA on the Net

http://www.ama-assn.org

The American Medical Association has a site on the Net. If you want to search for a doctor, it has over 650,000 MDs listed.

48
Media Studies Forum

http://www.mediastudies.org

This site has analysis of current events that might shed some light on world happenings for you.

49
Area Code Search

http://www.xmission.com/~americom/aclookup.html

Plug in an area code, and you will learn what city it is located in.

50
If Darwin Only Knew

http://www.officialdarwinawards.com/darwin.html

Charles Darwin would not be proud. These sad and funny stories fit into the category of survival of the fittest…or is that extinction?

51
Forbes

http://www.forbes.com

One of the major business publications on the Net.

52
Home Improvement

http://www.housenet.com

http://www.nari.org

These sites are for the home improvement person. You can even ask questions. So, Bob Vila and Tim Allen, the Net is catching up to you.

53
Traveling to a Foreign Country?

http://www.travlang.com

This site has a lot of valuable information about foreign travel. It also has a translation section that is quite interesting.

54
NFL

http://www.nfl.com

If you are a big football fan, this is a site you will not want to miss during the season.

55
He Gets Paid What?

http://www.paywatch.org

http://www.wageweb.com

Compare your salary to the compensation package of some of the big boys. For example, it might take you 2,000 years to earn what Disney's Michael Eisner made last year. Then learn at Wageweb what we regular folk earn.

56
Cost of Living

http://pathfinder.com/money/best-cities-97/seaindex.htm

http://woodrow.mpls.frb.fed.us/economy/calc/cpihome.html

Compare the cost of living in different cities. And since you are so curious, check out the cost of living in different years.

"I just joined a support group
for Internet addicts. We meet every night
from 7:00 until midnight on CompuServe."

57
Biography

http://www.biography.com

Have you ever watched Biography on TV? It is a great show. This site has a searchable database of 15,000 famous people.

58
Car Talk

http://www.cartalk.com

The famous brothers Tom and Ray have a lot of good automobile information on the Net.

59
Finance Center

http://www.financenter.com

This is an excellent site for credit card, automobile and home financing issues. It includes calculators for financial decisions.

60
Holiday Celebrations

http://www.holidays.net

Who doesn't love holidays? If it is on the Net, this site has it for you. Happy celebrating.

61
Currency Converter

http://www.traveloco.com/tools/xenon.html

http://www.dna.lth.se/cgi-bin/kurt/rates

These are easy-to-use currency conversion sites. If you're heading out of the country (or are just curious), check it out.

62
National Geographic

http://www.nationalgeographic.com

The famed foundation is now online. If you enjoy its detailed reporting on nature, science and the world around us, do not miss this site.

63
Inc. Magazine

http://www.inc.com

This magazine has long been a small business staple.

64
American City Business Journals

http://www.amcity.com

This site has major business publications in over 35 cities. You can even place your "business card" at this site for free.

65
Lawyers, Lawyers, Lawyers

http://www.martindale.com

http://www.wld.com

Every lawyer in the land is listed here.

66
Find the Best Rates

http://www.primerate.com
You can search for rates, fees and services for many financial products: credit cards, savings accounts, certificates of deposit and loans.

67
True or False?

http://www.cagle.com/art/3GovtTRUE.html
These are actual facts about the U.S. government, and Daryl Cagle has an interesting way of presenting the information.

68
News as Easy as 1, 2, 3

http://www.msnbc.com
http://www.abcnews.com
http://uttm.com
Get your news from the "big three" television networks.

69
The Sporting Life

http://www.sportsline.com
http://www.foxsports.com
http://www.espn.com
http://www.cnnsi.com
If you enjoy sports, do not miss out on these sites.

70
Real Estate on the Net

http://www.realtor.com
This site has over one million properties and a customized search capability for finding the home of your dreams.

71
Software Version Tracker

http://www.versiontracker.com
This straightforward site tells you the current versions of many software titles. There are also links to the vendors.

72
Looking for a Job?

http://www.monster.com
http://www.careermosaic.com
http://www.jobdirect.com
At these sites, you can look for a particular position, post a résumé and learn about other ways to use the Net for a job search.

73
Phone Numbers

http://www.infospace.com
You can say goodbye to the "dead-tree" version of the phone book. Take a look: This site has many treats.

74
Menus and Food Reviews

http://www.onlinemenus.com
http://www.pathfinder.com/travel/zagat
If you are hungry, check out a menu. Of course, check Zagat's restaurant reviews first.

75
ParentSoup

http://www.parentsoup.com

All parents have been in hot water. Let ParentSoup bail you out.

76
E-mail Discussion Group

http://www.liszt.com

Need to talk (e-mail) with someone about a specific topic? You can do it here.

77
The Motley Fool

http://www.fool.com

These guys are famous. Learn to beat the stock market from these fools.

78
U.S. House of Representatives Internet Law Library

http://law.house.gov/1.htm

Here's a directory of over 5,100 links to law resources on the Internet.

79
Daily E-mail Tips

http://www.tipworld.com

http://www.zdtips.com

If you want to get a tip a day for many software products, take this tip: Visit these sites.

80
Versions

http://www.versions.com

Do you need to know when a new software version occurs in a product that you use? Versions will e-mail you when an update of your software is available.

81
FindLaw

http://www.findlaw.com

http://www.catalaw.com

 If it has to do with law, no doubt you will find it here. From law schools to legal issues, A to W ("Anti-Trust" to "Woman").

82

The New York Federal Reserve Bank

http://www.ny.frb.org

This site has a lot of information, but the best is the bond calculator. If you have any Federal Bonds (EE), go here to find out their current value. In the past, you would have had to go to the bank.

83

My Virtual Reference Desk

http://www.refdesk.com

The Internet is the world's largest library, containing millions of books, artifacts, images, documents, maps, etc. This site will help you find it all.

84

Airline Reservations

http://www.travelocity.com

At this site, make airline reservations, check airfares, request the lowest price and a lot more.

85
CNN and CNNfn

http://www.cnn.com

http://www.cnnfn.com

http://customnews.cnn.com

Up-to-date news and financial information by the CNN group. Is Larry King out here somewhere?

86
The Word Detective

http://www.word-detective.com

Did you ever wonder where phrases like "lame duck" came from? Visit Word Detective for the answer.

87
Philosophy on the Net

http://www.phil.ruu.nl/philosophy-sites.html

We net-aholics know that the Internet is itself a philosophy. So why not check out philosophy on the Net?

88
RxList

http://www.rxlist.com

Is this your online pharmacist? No, but you can get a lot of information about various medications.

89
Maps of the World

http://pathfinder.com/Travel/maps/index.html

http://www.nationalgeographic.com/resources/ngo/maps

Good for the global village we live in; especially if you have any need or desire to see a map of anywhere in the world.

90
The Electronic Library

http://www.elibrary.com

This site lets you search for items that have been in articles in magazines, newspapers and more.

91
Emory Law School Web Site
http://www.law.emory.edu/FEDCTS
This site has legal opinions from all of the federal appellate courts and the Supreme Court, and it's free.

92
Salary Calculation
http://www.homefair.com/homefair/cmr/salcalc.html
Compare your current situation versus another. Cost-of-living issues and other stuff are at this site as well.

93
Get Healthy!
http://www.healthfinder.gov
http://www.healthatoz.com
http://www.yourhealth.com
http://www.yourhealth.com/ahl
These sites will assist you in living the healthy lifestyle. Don't forget: Turn off the Net, go outside, get some exercise and breathe the fresh air.

94
QuickQuote

http://www.quickquote.com

Use this site to buy insurance or just compare a quote with what you already have.

95
Science Surf

http://weber.u.washington.edu/~wcalvin/scisurf.html

William H. Calvin has an excellent science site with links to many other mind-expanding locations. If your thirst for knowledge is great, be prepared to stay a while.

96
Are You Addicted to the Net?

http://www.earthplaza.com/netaholics

You are not alone. Join some Internet friends at this site.

97
Sports Stadium and Arena Sites

http://www.wwcd.com/stadiums.html

http://www.ballparks.com

If you are a sports fanatic, check out these arena layouts and seating charts.

98
Mail That 'Toon

http://www.toonogram.com

Choose a cartoon from here to be e-mailed to someone with a note from you.

99
The New York Times

http://www.nytimes.com

Cuddle up to the screen and read the NYT to your heart's content.

100
Joe Boxer

http://www.joeboxer.com
Hold on to your shorts while you are at this creative, informative and funny site.

101
Consumer Issues

http://www.consumerworld.org
http://www.consumerreports.org
There are an amazing array of sites (over 1,500) that will help you with consumer-oriented issues at ConsumerWorld. When you are done there, visit Consumer Reports for even more valuable information.

102

Going Local

http://local.yahoo.com

http://www.sidewalk.com

http://www.digitalcity.com

http://www.divein.com

These sites have a lot of information about cities. If you are traveling, require information about a town or just have a need to know, dive right in.

103

MapBlaster

http://www.mapblast.com

This unique site allows you to create a map based on a street address that you provide. One unique feature is that you can then e-mail it to someone. Is a customer coming in from out of town? Let him know where you are located.

104
The NBA

http://www.nba.com
If you are a basketball fan, this is a site you will not want to miss.

105
Did They Really Say That?

http://www.comedybreak.com/quotes/index.htm
Here is an archive of things people have said that are so stupid they're funny.

106
Business Week

http://www.businessweek.com
Read all about business at the Business Week site. You can even subscribe to a weekly e-mail reminder.

107
Travel

http://expedia.msn.com
Microsoft's Expedia is an excellent source of travel information and services.

108
Zippy Directions

http://www.zip2.com

Get the most detailed driving directions on the Net. Also, find out a lot about any city in the U.S.

109
Law Research

http://www.lawresearch.com

Lawyers, this is for you. Actually, any businessperson should take a look at the many good links at this site.

110
Premier Source for Mortgage Info!

http://www.hsh.com

http://www.homeowners.com

Two excellent sites for home mortgage information, mortgage calculators and much more.

111
Where in the World?

http://www.astro.ch/atlas

If you need to know where any city in the world is located, this is the place to check it out.

112
Yack, Yack, Yack

http://www.yack.com

Do you like to yack? Here is the ultimate site on the Net for chat rooms on a wide variety of topics.

113
What Sites Do You Like?

http://www.firefly.com

Let Firefly help you find sites that are your cup of tea.

"Thank you for calling. Please leave a message.
In case I forget to check my messages, please
send your message as an audio file to my e-mail,
then send me a fax to remind me to check my
e-mail, then call back to remind me to
check my fax."

114
The Inc. 500

http://www.inc.com/500

Not a car race, this is Inc. magazine's annual list of the 500 fastest-growing companies.

115
Movie Buff

http://www.allmovie.com

http://www.moviebuff.com

http://www.movieweb.com

http://www.boxoff.com

Everything you ever wanted to know about movies can be found at these sites.

116
The Platinum Rule

http://www.platinumrule.com

Everyone knows the Golden Rule: "Do unto others as you would have them do unto you." The real key to success may be to apply the Platinum Rule: "Do unto others as they would like done unto them!"

117
BankRate

http://www.bankrate.com

At this site there is a tremendous amount of personal financial information: mortgage, equity loan, credit card, rates of all kinds and a lot more.

118
Road Trip!

http://www.freetrip.com

http://www.delorme.com/cybermaps/cyberrouter.htm

http://www.mapsonus.com

These sites work a lot like the CD-ROM Automap. Just put in your starting point (e.g., Atlanta, GA) and your ending destination (e.g., Charleston, SC) and you will get detailed directions.

119
Play the Market

http://www.investorsleague.com

Get $100,000 "play money" to invest in the stock market. This Stock Market Simulator is from the League of American Investors. It offers one of the most effective methods to learn about investing.

120
Baseball Fanatics

http://www.baseballstats.com

http://www.totalbaseball.com

If you really love baseball, check these two sites out. They have statistics and records galore and can help settle a few friendly bets.

121
A Drum Roll, Please

http://pathfinder.com/ew/970418/feature/funny-people/funny2.html

Who are the 50 funniest people alive? Find out here.

122
I Will, I Will

http://www.ca-probate.com/wills.htm

Curious about who and what's in the wills of Jerry Garcia, Richard Nixon, John Lennon, Jackie O. and others? This site has them all.

123
Good News

http://www.positivepress.com
I don't know about you, but I get tired of watching and listening to predominantly negative reporting. It's refreshing to read the positive news here.

124
Scrabble

http://yoda.cs.udw.ac.za/~ns2
Play scrabble against people from all over the world.

125
Over Achiever

http://www.achievement.org
If there were a site titled "Overachievers Anonymous," this would be it. This site has people who have been successful in business, the arts, entertainment, sports and more.

126
Young Bucks

http://www.younginvestor.com
Monetary issues for teenagers.

127
Universities on the Net

http://www.clas.ufl.edu/CLAS/american-universities.html
Use this site to access the web pages of colleges and universities throughout the world.

128
Greetings Everyone

http://www.xenus.com/postcard/age.htm
http://www.bytesizegreetings.com/cards.html
There are many greeting sites on the Net; these will get you started. Go ahead send a friend or a loved one a "virtual greeting."

129
The Fortune 500
http://pathfinder.com/fortune/fortune500/500list.html
The well-known index of powerful companies. Number one is General Motors at $168 billion.

130
What Time is It?
http://tycho.usno.navy.mil/what.html
http://www.arachnoid.com/lutusp/worldclock.htm
You'll never ask that question again. These sites tell you the time all over the world.

131
Ecola
http://www.ecola.com
This very impressive Web site allows you to search for technology companies, universities and publications. Searches are quick, and innovative features are provided.

132

Research It!

http://www.itools.com/research-it/research-it.html

If you seek something on the subjects of: language, geography, finance, shipping & mailing, famous quotes or a lot more, check out this worthwhile site.

133

Movies in Your Town

http://www.movielink.com

Find out which movies are playing at your local theater.

134

Headliner

http://www.headliner.com

News junkies: Headliner delivers to you from an incredible number of sources.

135
Park Search

http://www.llbean.com/parksearch

http://www.nps.gov

Thank you LL Bean and the U.S. government. These sites have over 900 USA parks in their database.

136
Virtual Flowers

http://www.virtualflowers.com/vflower_select.phtml

They may not smell as good as real flowers, but they are cheaper (free), get there faster and the card says exactly what you want it to say.

137
Be My Buddy

http://www.aol.com

Send an instant message to friends who are online. America Online's excellent "Buddy List" software is available to anyone on the Net.

138
Hot Coupons

http://www.hotcoupons.com

Are you a coupon clipper? Just go to this site, put in your zip code and you will get coupons to use at various establishments.

139
Internet News

http://www.newshub.com

http://www.newslinx.com

These sites are excellent for obtaining technology news stories from some of the major publications on the Net. They allow you to scan titles and decide if you want to read the stories.

140
Profusion Search Engine

http://topaz.designlab.ukans.edu/profusion

This search engine does an excellent job using Alta Vista, Excite, InfoSeek, Lycos, OpenText and WebCrawler as the bases for its search.

141
Computer ESP

http://www.computeresp.com
Indexes over 400,000 entries from computer cyberstores so that you can easily find up-to-date computer prices.

142
Liven Up Your E-mail

http://st-www.cs.uiuc.edu/users/chai/figlet.html
http://users.inetw.net/~mullen/ascii.htm
http://www.info.polymtl.ca/ada2/tranf/www/asciiarts.html
Create text effects to use in e-mail with Figlet, and become an artist with ASCII art.

143
Doctors On Call

http://www.doctorsoncall.com
Doctors On Call (DOC) is the largest medical professional directory on the Web. Search for a medical professional from a list of 400,000 U.S. doctors.

144
Business Traveler

http://www.biztravel.com

If you travel on business, check this site out. You can track flights in progress, learn about cities throughout the world, get directions, obtain your frequent flyer miles (not all airlines are available) and a lot of other stuff.

145
Mortgage Net

http://www.mortgage-net.com

http://mortgage.quicken.com

Here are the ultimate mortgage sites. There are historical and current rates and tons of other stuff. If you're in the home market, camp out here for a while.

146
Moving?

http://www.movequest.com

If you are moving or just want to know about another city (worldwide coverage), check this site out. There are many interesting features, such as a salary calculator.

147
City Guides

http://cityguide.lycos.com
The Lycos city guide has detailed information about cities in: Australia, Canada, Europe, Ireland, New Zealand, United Kingdom and United States.

148
Ask Dr. Web

http://www.zeldman.com/faq4f.html
Dr. Web wants you to have a well-designed site. He offers some very candid and thought-provoking suggestions on how to make a Web site all it can be.

149
10, 9, 8...1

http://www.cbs.com/lateshow/ttlist.html
David Letterman's Top Ten lists have become legend. Now you can read them all the way back to 1993.

150
Matchmaker, Matchmaker

http://www.mylaunch.com

http://www.reel.com

Let these sites help you identify music and movies that are to your liking.

151
TV Guide

http://www.tvguide.com

Yes, you can get your TV Guide online.

152
Patents Galore

http://www.ibm.com/patent

IBM lets you access over 26 years of U.S. Patent & Trademark Office patent descriptions as well as the last ten years of images. The first entries date back to January 5, 1971. You can search, retrieve and study over two million patents.

153
Politically Incorrect

http://eyescream.com/callahan

No, not the TV show. If you are tired of all this politically correct stuff, then take a look at John Callahan's cartoons. Guaranteed not to be politically correct.

154
Randy Glasbergen

http://www.norwich.net/~randyg/toon.html

Randy's cartoons are used in this book. Check his site out: He is guaranteed to make you laugh.

155
PBS

http://www.pbs.org

If you enjoy the high quality of programming on PBS (TV), then no doubt you will enjoy PBS Online. And if you want a weekly update, get on the e-mail update list.

156
'Toon Time

http://www.cagle.com/art/main.asp
Every cartoonist on the Net is listed here.

157
Money Talks

http://www.talks.com
You bet it does. Money Talks, written by well-respected financial writers, is a magazine for serious individual investors.

158
Map That Data

http://maps.esri.com/ESRI/mapobjects/tmap.htm
Now you can take census data and make a colorful map out of it.

159
A Lot of News

http://www.inkling.com
http://www.newsworks.com
http://www.totalnews.com

Knight-Ridder (Inkling) has 27 papers on the Net; Newsworks is a group of 125 major newspapers; and Total News contains many major publications with a lot of links to great news, sports, entertainment, opinion sites and an interesting search capability.

160
Push Technology

http://form.netscape.com/ibd/cgi-bin/ibd-x.cgi

The concept of receiving Web sites via e-mail is the only way to go. Netscape has some innovative technology.

161
FAA Online

http://www.faa.gov
The Federal Aviation Agency is now required to provide safety records and other pertinent information about airlines at its Web site.

162
Inventor's Hall of Fame

http://www.invent.org/book/index.html
And you thought the Hall of Fame was for sports heroes. Check out these smart folks who have invented a lot of incredible stuff.

163
Vanity E-mail

http://mailbank.com
http://www.iname.com
These sites have an incredible amount of e-mail addresses. So, if you are not satisfied with the one you have—check it out.

164
Money Online's Ultimate Guide to Mutual Funds

http://pathfinder.com/money/funds/index.html

Pathfinder allows you to search a comprehensive database of 3,400 funds to find the ones that best fit your investment objectives.

165
Gifts

http://www.giftone.com

http://www.webistry.com

Order a gift online for a loved one. They will also remind you of important dates that you provide. And while you're at it, go ahead and register for gifts at the Webistry.

166
Trivia on the Net

http://www.trivia.net

If you are a trivia fan, check out Trivia.net. There are thousands of questions, such as: "What famous comedian was once convicted of smuggling and fined $10,000—Bob Hope, Jimmy Durante, Jack Benny or George Burns? Here's a hint: think violin.

167
Lycos Finds the Stock Market

http://www.stockfind.newsalert.com

Lycos, the search engine, is branching out. At this site you can get market updates, search for stocks and get business articles during the day.

168
Franchise and More

http://www.bison1.com

Bison stands for: Business International Sales and Opportunity Network. It has a great search engine to identify franchise opportunities.

169
Having My Baby

http://www.olen.com/baby

The Interactive Pregnancy Calendar will build a day-by-day customized calendar detailing the development of a baby from before conception to birth.

"My History professor told me to use the Internet
for research and it's been very helpful.
I've located seventeen people who have
offered to sell me a term paper!"

170
The Mining Company

http://miningco.com
This site is broken down into; health, sports, news, business and more. You will find some golden sites here, so get your shovel and wade through.

171
Uncle Sam

http://www.uncle-sam.com
http://www.capweb.net
A Citizen's Guide to the treasures of the U.S. Government on the World Wide Web.

172
Stroud's Consummate Internet Software

http://www.stroud.com
This can be your one-stop shopping site for the latest and greatest Internet software.

173
DLJDirect
http://www.dljdirect.com

At DLJDirect you can get current stock market information and track your portfolio. The most powerful feature is obtaining news reports, press releases and regulatory information about companies.

174
Search the World
http://www.personalseek.com/seek/search.htm

This site contains search engines from A to U ("Austria" to "United States"). This is just another interesting example of information search on the Net.

175
Mortgage Prepayment Calculator
http://www.bloomberg.com/cgi-bin/ilpc.cgi

This is a quick and easy-to-use mortgage calculator, compliments of Bloomberg. You can identify how prepayment will affect your mortgage payoff.

176
Mind Your Money With the Instant Budget Maker

http://pathfinder.com/cgi-bin/Money/instant.cgi

How does your spending compare to that of others? Find out with MONEY Online's Instant Budget Maker. A simple way to analyze your spending habits.

177
USA Today

http://www.usatoday.com

Of course, the popular weekday "paper."

178
GolfWeb

http://www.golfweb.com

GolfWeb has an excellent golf site. If you are a golfer, go here right now.

179
Auto Information Overload

http://www.autotown.com

http://www.alldata.com

When it comes to autos, Autown has it all, and Alldata will tell you the repair and recall record for most cars.

180
AltaVista

http://www.altavista.digital.com

AltaVista has made searching the Net a lot easier. After the initial search, use the "refine icon" to include or exclude words from the search.

181
Hot Off the Press

http://www.nytimes.com/aponline

Breaking news updates from A.P. are now available every ten minutes at The New York Times on the Web.

182
The Megalist

http://www.2020tech.com/submit.html
Here is a site that should be helpful in identifying sites that will list your site.

183
Audit Bait

http://pathfinder.com/money/features/auditbait_0196/auditindex.html
The IRS seems to have a spell on the U.S. public—compliance by intimidation. This site will allow you to see if the IRS may have you squirming like a fish.

184
Legal Documents

http://www.legaldocs.com
This creative legal site offers an interactive preparation service for many legal documents.

185
Federal Election Commission

http://www.tray.com/fecinfo

A place to discover who gave what to which political candidates.

186
1,001 Web Tips

http://www.zdnet.com/pccomp/besttips

PC Computing, in a valiant effort, provides 1,001 tips to help in using the Net.

187
Can We Chat?

http://chat.yahoo.com

"Chat rooms" are very popular on the Net; jump in at this site.

188
Have You Heard the One About?

http://www.nolo.com/jokes/jokes.html

Everyone loves a good lawyer joke. Load up for the next cocktail party at this site.

189
Music Lyrics

http://www.lyrics.ch

This site has the words to over 40,000 songs in inventory.

190
Truckin' Down the Information Highway

http://www.deadradio.com

Oh excuse me, I better get back to work. This is a 24-hour, 7-day-a-week, RealAudio site that plays only the Grateful Dead.

191
Buydirect.com

http://www.buydirect.com

A convenient location for purchasing and downloading software. The Internet's leading software applications are available here at manufacturer's prices.

192
Stock Direct

http://www.netstockdirect.com

Now you can buy stocks directly from the companies. Yes, that is correct—no broker commissions.

193
U.S. Presidents' Tax Returns

http://www.taxhistory.org/presidential

In case you have an inquiring mind, you might want to see the actual tax returns of some recent U.S. presidents.

194

Mortgage Rates Constantly Updated

http://www.microsurf.com

A very useful site for finding out mortgage rates. It also has mortgage calculators.

195

Board Certified

http://certifieddoctor.org/verify.html

It seems like many people are afraid to ask their doctors if they are Board Certified. Well, don't ask. Just go to this site to find out.

196

CNN City Guides

http://www.cnn.com/TRAVEL/CITY.GUIDES

Get a map of just about any city in the world. You can also obtain specific details about many cities.

197
Everybody Sells

http://salesdoctors.com/misc/index.htm
The Sales Doctor has a lot of information for the sales professional.

198
Are You a Millionaire?

http://www.lottonet.com
What are the winning lottery numbers? If you win, please remember me!

199
IPO ABCs

http://www.ipocentral.com
http://www.ipodata.com
If you are interested in Initial Public Offerings, then IPO Central and IPO Data are your locations.

200
Family Doctor

http://www.familydr.com/exam
http://www.familydr.com/pharmacy
These two sites allow you to get basic information about ailments and prescription drugs.

201
May I Recommend...

http://www.recomentor.com
The Top 10, this is the "ultimate measure of popular culture." Go to this site now and have some fun. It has every area of our culture covered.

202
The Royal Family

http://www.royal.gov.uk
The British Royal family has gone online.

203
The Dow Jones Industrial Average

http://www.dbc.com/cgi-bin/htx.exe/dbcfiles/dowt.html?SOURCE=/BLQ/HOOVERS

http://www.dogsofthedow.com

Who are the companies that make up the famous index? And read about an interesting investment strategy at Dogs of the Dow.

204
Ask the Builder

http://www.askbuild.com

Tim Carter has an excellent site. You can ask him any question about your home and read the articles that he writes about home projects.

205
It's Happening Here

http://www.eventcal.com

Go to Event Calendar and you will definitely know what is going on. You will be able to search by city, state or venue. There are over 500,000 events in the database.

206
Tax Time

http://www.fourmilab.ch/ustax/ustax.html
During these taxing times, you might want to check out the tax code (all 6,000 pages of it). Happy filing.

207
Love Gone Bad

http://www.divorcenet.com
http://www.divorcesource.com
There is a lot of talk about love on the Net, but the reality is that over 50% of the U.S. population gets divorced.

208
Ancestors

http://www.ancestry.com
This is your place for genealogy on the Web. Type in a name, and see what you can find out.

209
Calorie Conscious

http://www.caloriecontrol.org

http://www.dietitian.com

Fat: The great American obsession. These two sites will keep you fit and trim.

210
Package Tracking with UPS and FedEx

http://www.ups.com/tracking/tracking.html

http://www.fedex.com/track_it.html

Track a package that was sent via UPS or FedEx.

211
Remind Me

http://www.netmind.com/html/register.html

If you want to be reminded when a Web site is updated, this site will keep you informed.

212

Vitamins

http://pathfinder.com/thrive/health/vitamin.chart.html

Pathfinder has a concise site that provides good information about vitamins.

213

Beanie Babies

http://www.ty.com

http://www.beaniemom.com

The Official Web site of Beanie Babies. This is an excellent example of engaging kids in one of their passions. You can even print out the entire list of every Beanie Baby ever "born!" Also, visit the Beanie Mom. Are you one?

214

Demographics Galore

http://www.easidemographics.com/easi_free_reports.html

If you need a little or a lot of information about a specific geographic area, you can get it here.

215
The Big Apple

http://www.nycvisit.com/home.html

The official tourism Web Site of the New York Convention & Visitors Bureau.

216
The Internet For Real People

http://www.thebee.com/bweb/brand.htm

http://www.creativegood.com/help/index.html

http://www.webnovice.com

There are many people on the Net who think simplicity is a thing of beauty. These sites try to simplify the Net for all.

217
Simple Web Address

http://this.is

http://surf.to

If you want to simplify or customize the address (URL) of your Web site, go here. By the way, the people who provide these services are located in Iceland and Tonga, respectively.

218
Earnings Report

http://pathfinder.com/money/moneydaily/1997/970321a.moneyonline.html
At Pathfinder's site are listed over 3,300 publicly-traded companies, with their stock symbol and when their annual earnings will be announced.

219
Search Major Newspapers

http://www.nytimes.com/search/daily
New York Times

http://167.8.29.8/plweb-cgi/ixacct.pl
USA Today

http://www.washingtonpost.com/wp-srv/searches/mainsrch.htm
Washington Post

http://www.LATimes.com/HOME/ARCHIVES/simple.htm
Los Angeles Times

220
Newsalert

http://www.newsalert.com
This site provides you with news, information, SEC filings, stock quotes and other information. You can even download a very fine stock ticker.

221
StockSmart

http://www.stocksmart.com/ows-bin/owa/cact.g
Visit this site to learn about: upcoming stock splits, distributions and corporate dividends.

222
Ask ERIC

http://ericir.syr.edu
ERIC actually stands for Educational Resources Information Center. This is a federally-funded national information system that provides a variety of services and products on a broad range of education-related issues.

223
Ignorance is Stupidity

http://www.atr.org/atr/calculator/html/start.html

If you are a U.S. taxpayer, go to this site NOW. This site will depress you, but the Net is here to give you knowledge. Find out what a poor investment the Social Security tax is. You can do an actual calculation here.

224
Social Security Administration

http://www.ssa.gov

The SSA has a very pretty page. You can request your SS benefits at this site. Go for it.

225
Can't Find That Station

http://www.radioguide.com/cities.html

Every time you visit a new city, you probably have to fumble around to find the radio stations that you like. Well, here are complete listings in the top 100 markets in the U.S.

"My husband passed away eight
months ago, but we still keep in touch.
His e-mail address is WalterZ@Heaven.com"

226
Road Construction

http://www.randmcnally.com/tools/construc.htm
Before you head off on that next road trip, check this site out to see if there is any construction going on along the way. There are also many other interesting sites to see while touring this one.

227
The Library of Congress

http://lcweb.loc.gov
It's huge, and it's also on the Net. Your taxes pay for it, so take advantage of all the information.

228
C|Net

http://www.cnet.com
One of the best sources for anything related to the Internet.

229
DejaNews

http://www.dejanews.com
If you need to find something in a "newsgroup," this is your place to go.

230
Reference

http://www.reference.com
Reference allows you to search newsgroups by type of "conversation." You can find a lot of good information by using this site. Of course, you can also find a lot of junk.

231
Culture Vulture

http://www.culturefinder.com
If you are in the "upper crust" of society, by all means check out Culturefinder. You can search for all those cultural events.

232
Golf Search

http://www.golfsearch.com

Sorry, this site will not find your lost ball, but it will tell you where to find golf-related items on the Net.

233
Famous Quotes

http://www.cc.columbia.edu/acis/bartleby/bartlett

http://www.starlingtech.com/quotes

You can find most of them here. You can quote me on that.

234
Business Directory

http://businessdirectory.dowjones.com

Here's what they say: "Your guide to high quality business Web sites." Guess what? It has accurate and good business information without getting overloaded.

235
Happy Birthday

http://www.scopesys.com/anyday
http://www.440.com/twtd/today.html
http://www.historychannel.com/thisday
http://www.thehistorynet.com/today/today.htm
Who was born? Who died? And what else happened on this day? Find out here.

236
College Sports

http://www.FANSonly.com
If you enjoy college sports, this site was designed for you.

237
All the Hotels on the Web

http://www.all-hotels.com
Over 10,000 of them. Sleep tight.

238
Airlines on the Web

http://w1.itn.net/airlines

If it isn't at this site, then it doesn't fly. Happy travels.

239
Concerts

http://www.pollstar.com

If you want to go to a concert, this is your site to find any concert, anywhere, anytime.

240
Play Ball

http://www.majorleaguebaseball.com

http://www.fastball.com

Here are two great sites to follow Major League Baseball.

241
That's Show Business

http://www.mrshowbiz.com
http://www.eonline.com
No doubt, these sites will keep you entertained.

242
Rock and Roll Hall of Fame

http://www.rockhall.com
The Net rocks at the Rock and Roll Hall of Fame.

243
Epicurious

http://www.epicurious.com
If it has to do with food and drink, it will be here.

244
Let's Talk

http://www.vocaltec.com

The Net provides free telephone calls all over the world.

245
Political Index

http://www.politicalindex.com

This is an index of a tremendous amount of political information.

246
Presidential Biographies

http://ipl.sils.umich.edu/ref/POTUS

They are all here, from Washington to Clinton.

247
The White House

http://www.whitehouse.gov

Yes, the one at 1600 Pennsylvania Avenue.

248
Congress on the Net

http://thomas.loc.gov

In the spirit of Thomas Jefferson, a service of the U.S. Congress through its Library.

249
Product Review

http://www.productreviewnet.com

Type in a product category, and find out about the product.

250
Insurance

http://www.life-line.org/fit_home.html

Straightforward and unbiased information on insurance—life and health.

251
You First

http://www.youfirst.com

Taking control of your health begins with a better understanding of factors discussed here.

252

Grammar and Style

http://www.english.upenn.edu/~jlynch/Grammar

Most of us can use some assistance with our use of the English language. Ain't that the truth!

253

Cost of Living

http://www.NewsEngin.com/neFreeTools.nsf/CPIcalc

Ah, the good old days. Compare today's cost of living with any other year.

254

Simple Math

http://www.NewsEngin.com/neFreeTools.nsf/PercentChange/formPercentChange

http://www.worldwidemetric.com/metcal.htm

http://www.cchem.berkeley.edu/ChemResources/temperature.html

Many of us have trouble with percentage change, the Metric System and Fahrenheit to Celsius conversions. Have no fear; these sites will keep you cool and calm.

255
Home Life

http://www.livinghome.com

If you have a house, you will need all the resources this site has: home calculators, gardening tips and a host of other things.

256
Mortgage, Finance Calculators and More

http://alfredo.wustl.edu/mort_links.html

http://homepage.interaccess.com/~wolinsky/measure.htm

All kinds of different calculators. If a calculator is on the Net, you'll find it here.

257
Shareware for Everyone

http://www.shareware.com

http://www.jumbo.com

http://filepile.com

Millions of software programs are waiting for you to download. Try one of these sites out.

258
Magazines Galore

http://www.enews.com

If you want to find a magazine on the Net, it will probably be here.

259
The Small Business Association

http://www.sbaonline.sba.gov

The SBA has a tremendous amount of resource information for any business.

260
Yahoo!

http://www.yahoo.com

The best-known search directory on the Net.

261
Let's Talk Business

http://www.biztalk.com

Biztalk has a large amount of information for those with small businesses.

262
Legal Information Institute

http://www.law.cornell.edu/lii.table.html

Cornell Law School provides an incredible amount of legal resources here.

263
New York Times Book Review

http://www.nytimes.com/books

Over 50,000 books are reviewed at this site.

264
NHL

http://www.nhl.com

Hockey…the official site of the National Hockey League.

265
Weather Fans

http://www.weather.com
http://live.excite.com/?weather
http://www.wunderground.com

Everyone's favorite topic of conversation. With these sites, you won't be left out in the cold.

266
The Internet Sleuth

http://www.isleuth.com

This site will search over 2,000 different databases for you.

267
C|Net's Search

http://www.search.com

It isn't called search.com for nothing. This will help you find any number of things on the Net.

268
Games and Things

http://www.gamecenter.com
If games are your thing, check out the game center.

269
Find an Old Friend (or a new one)

http://www.four11.com
http://www.whowhere.com
http://www.accumail.com
http://www.bigfoot.com
http://www.switchboard.com
Find anyone's e-mail address by using these information search engines.

270
Business Research

http://www.brint.com
If research is your thing, make a stop at Business Research in Information and Technology. You won't be disappointed.

271
Talk Internet

http://www.annonline.com
http://www.pcworld.com/news/newsradio/feature_archive.html
Ann Devlin and Brian McWilliams conduct great interviews on the Net. Ann chats with an interesting personality every weekday, and Brian concentrates on technology issues.

272
50 Something

http://www.thirdage.com
Third Age is a site that addresses the needs and concerns of the baby boomer generation. If that's you, this might be a good place for you to hang out.

273
Fashion and Style

http://www.firstview.com
If fashion is your passion, this is the site for you. All of the major designers are here with pictures of their current creations.

274
Yahoo! Takes Off

http://yahoo.flifo.com

Yahoo is now in the travel business. Yep, you can book flights and find out arrival and departure times.

275
Teledesic

http://www.teledesic.com

It's a bird, it's a plane no…it's Internet access brought to you via satellite.

276
Learn 2

http://www.learn2.com

A fascinating place where you can learn to do almost anything.

277
Zip Code Lookup

http://www.westminster.ca/cdnlook.htm

Do you need to know the zip code for an address? This is the location.

278

Phone Number = Name and Address

http://www.cedar.buffalo.edu/AdServ/person-search.html

Do you have a phone number but don't have the corresponding name or address? With this site, you have it all.

279

The Tax Foundation

http://www.taxfoundation.org

Learn a lot about your tax dollar. For example, the "average" American works until May 9th to pay his tax bill.

280

SIC Code Lookup

http://www.osha.gov/oshstats/sicser.html

Find out what the SIC classification is for any business.

281
Hoovers

http://www.hoovers.com

Proclaims itself as "the ultimate source for company information on the Net."

282
The Stock Market

http://www.nyse.com

http://www.nasdaq.com

http://www.amex.com

All of the major stock markets are waiting for you.

283
Brief News on Your Desktop

http://www.msnbc.com/toolkit.asp

Let MSNBC "push" news and information to your desktop. It provides brief summaries of a variety of stories and features. If a particular item interests you, click on it and go directly to the Web site.

284
Ask Jeeves, and He'll Find It

http://www.askjeeves.com
You simply ask "Jeeves" a question, and he will (amazingly) find the correct answer for you. Most of the time, he is right on target. He can also find things you never would have thought of. Amazing!

285
Internet Demographics

http://www.cyberatlas.com
There is not really a good "handle" on demographics on the Net, but Cyberatlas attempts to give us some indication of what is happening.

286
Autoresponder

http://www.mailback.com
Autoresponders are something like "Fax-on-Demand" but are easier to use and much more powerful. This site allows you to set up an autoresponder.

287
The Gadget Guru

http://www.gadgetguru.com/aol

If there is a product that you are thinking of buying, visit the guru. Maybe he has reviewed it. It has a search engine that makes it easy to find stuff.

288
Submit It

http://www.submit-it.com

Everyone with a Web site wants it to be known by the search engines. This site will let you register your site quickly.

289
Your Web Page

http://lycos.dialweb.com/entry

http://www.yahoo.com/docs/yahootogo/index.html

Here are some sites that let you place some good stuff on your Web page: your voice, a search engine and maps. Go for it; it's all free.

290
Shake It Up Baby

http://www.webtender.com

http://www.idrink.com

Let's make a toast. If you want to know anything about a mixed drink, these are your sites.

291
Sports Network

http://www.sportsnetwork.com

Most of the sports are covered here, and you can view live scoreboards for many. It's a sports fan's dream come true.

292
60 Greatest Conspiracies

http://www.conspire.com

Conspiracy theories are big now. Read all about the "60 Greatest."

293
Travel Source

http://www.travelsource.com
http://www.frommers.com
http://www.fodors.com
Are you a serious traveler? If so, then don't leave home without them.

294
The Farmers Almanac

http://www.almanac.com
The one and only.

295
Meet EDGAR

http://www.sec.gov/edgarhp.htm
Electronic Data Gathering, Analysis, and Retrieval system—performs automated collection, validation, indexing, acceptance and forwarding of submissions by companies and others who are required by law to file forms with the U.S. Securities and Exchange Commission.

296
Listen Up

http://www.timecast.com

There are literally thousands of things you can listen to on the Net using RealAudio. This is a good starting point.

297
Film

http://www.film.com

Get current information about the film industry—reviews and more.

298
Healthcare

http://www.achoo.com

http://www.phys.com

http://healthanswers.com

http://www.healthyideas.com

You can never be too healthy. Here are some sites that will help insure your health

299
My, Oh My

http://my.yahoo.com

http://my.excite.com

My these are excellent sites! Get all your news and information from one Web page. You can even customize it for your own needs. Make sure you use one for your "start page."

300
10Laughs

http://obryan.com/10Laughs

Just so you can finish this book with a smile, check out 10Laughs.

INDEX (BY SITE NUMBER)

Automobiles
Autotown: 179
Auto-By-Tel (car purchase): 23
Car Talk: 58
CarPoint: 5
Edmunds (car price): 5
Kelley Blue Book: 5
Lease vs. Purchase: 22
Business
Business Web Site: 234
Trade Shows and Events: 36, 205
Calendars/Reminders/Time
Exact Time: 130
Chat Rooms
Yack: 112
Yahoo!: 187
Comedy
All Cartoonists: 156
Addicted to the Net: 96
Joe Boxer: 100
Daryl Cagle (government): 67
John Callahan: 153
Darwin Awards: 50
Did They Really Say That?: 105
Dilbert: 35
E-mail a Cartoon: 98
Fifty Funniest People: 121
Lawyer Jokes: 188
Randy Glasbergen: 154
Ten Laughs: 300

Comedy (cont.)
Trivia: 166
Computers/Software
Buy Direct (price shopping): 191
Internet Software: 172
Product Pricing: 141
Shareware: 257
Version Tracker: 71
Versions: 80
Year 2000: 46
E-mail
Art: 142
Autoresponder: 286
E-mail to Fax: 28
Flowers by E-mail: 136
Juno: 8
Newsgroups: 76, 229, 230
Push Technology (Netscape): 160
Search: 269
Text Effects: 142
Tips: 79
Vanity Addresses: 163
Education
Ask Eric: 222
Colleges on the Net: 127
Employment
CareerMosaic: 72
Monster: 72
Entertainment
Alcoholic Beverages: 290

Entertainment (cont.)
Books: 18, 19, 263
Eonline: 241
Mr. Showbiz: 241
Retrospective: 42
Ticketmaster: 21
Family
Baby Calendar: 169
Parenting: 75
Fashion
Fashion and Style: 273
Financial, Corporate
Edgar: 295
Financial Statements: 11
Forbes 400: 34
Fortune 500: 129
Franchises: 168
Hoovers: 281
Inc. 500: 114
Street Eye: 33
Financial, Personal
Audit Bait: 183
Bank Rate: 117
Budget Maker: 176
Consumer World: 101
Cost of Living: 56, 253
Coupons: 138
Federal Reserve Board: 82
Gadget Guru: 287
Finance Center: 59

INDEX (BY SITE NUMBER)

Financial, Personal (cont.)
Insurance Information: 250
Insurance Quote: 94
Lottery: 198
Prime Rate: 66
Product Review: 249
Salary Comparison: 92
Salary of CEOs: 55
Salary of Regular Folk: 55
Social Security Investment: 223
Tax Code: 206
Food
Epicurious: 243
Menus Online: 74
Games/Toys
Beanie Babies: 213
Gamecenter: 268
Scrabble: 124
Government/Politics
All Politics: 25
Census: 14
Compare Political Views: 26
Congress: 248
FAA: 161
Federal Election Commission: 185
House Law Library: 78
Inaugural Speeches: 24
Leaders of the World: 20
Library of Congress: 227
National Debt: 16

Government/Politics (cont.)
Political Index: 245
Presidents' Tax Returns: 193
Royal Family (Britain): 202
Small Business Administration: 259
Social Security Administration: 224
Uncle Sam (gov. resources): 171
White House: 247
Grammar
Grammar and Style: 252
Word Detective: 86
Health, Medicine, Age Issues
Achoo: 298
AMA: 47
Board Certified: 195
Calories: 209
Dietician: 209
Doctors on Call: 143
Family Doctor: 200
Health Education: 251
Health Resources: 93, 298
Medications: 88
Third Age: 272
Vitamins: 212
Holidays and Occasions
Greeting Cards: 128
Holidays on the Net: 60
Internet Help/Tools
Demographics: 285
Firefly: 113

Internet Help/Tools (cont.)
Free Phone Calls: 244
Internet for Real People: 216
PBS Internet for Newbies: 38
Site Submittal: 182, 288
Teledesic: 275
URL: 217
Voice on a Web Page: 289
Web Site Design: 148
Web Site Reminder: 211
Web Tips: 186
Legal
Divorce: 207
Emory Law Library: 91
Findlaw (Legal Issues): 81
Law Research: 109
Lawyers (All of Them): 65
Legal Documents: 184
Legal Institute: 262
Maps
Census Data: 158
Mapblaster (Maps by Location): 103
Maps of the World: 89
Marketing
Demographics: 214
Sales Doctor: 197
Movies/TV
Film.com: 297
Movie Buff: 115
Movie Database: 17

Index (by site number)

Movies/TV (cont.)
Movie Recommendations: 201
Movie Selection: 150
Movies In Your Town: 133
TV Guide: 151
Music
Concerts: 239
Grateful Dead (24-hour music): 190
Music Lyrics: 189
Music Search (Time/Warner): 149
Radio Stations: 225
Rock and Roll Hall of Fame: 242
News and Information
CNN/CNNfn: 85
C/Net: 228
Headliner: 134
Infobeat: 4
Knight-Ridder: 159
Los Angeles Times: 219
Media Studies: 48
MSNBC: 68, 283
Newshub/Newslinx (Tech. News): 139
N.Y. Times: 99, 181, 219, 263
Newspapers All Over the World: 31
PBS: 155
PointCast: 2
Snap: 299
TotalNews: 159
USA Today: 177, 219
Washington Post: 45, 219

People
Achievement.org: 125
Biography: 57
Birthdays and more: 235
Birthday Calendar: 30
Inventor's Hall of Fame: 162
David Letterman: 149
Presidential Biographies: 246
Elvis Presley: 35
Quotes: 233
Martha Stewart: 35
Wills of Famous People: 122
Psychology and Philosophy
IQ and Personality Tests: 40
Platinum Rule: 116
Philosophy: 87
Publications, Financial
BizTalk: 261
Business Week: 106
Forbes: 51
Fortune: 10
Money Talks: 157
Wall Street Journal: 9
Publications, Magazines
Amcity Business Journals: 64
Consumer Reports: 101
E-news: 258
Farmer's Almanac: 294
Inc.: 63
National Geographic: 62

Publications, Magazines (cont.)
Pathfinder (Time/Warner): 10
RealAudio
Ann Devlin: 271
Grateful Dead (24-hour music): 190
Brian McWilliams: 271
RealAudio: 3
TimeCast (RealAudio Sites): 296
Real Estate/Home/Mortgage
Ask the Builder: 204
Home Improvement: 52
Home Resources: 255
Mortgage Info.: 110, 145, 194, 256
Mortgage Prepayment: 175
MoveQuest: 146
Realtor.com: 70
Reference/Research
Business: 270
Conspiracies: 292
Dictionaries: 39, 44
Ecola: 131
E-Library: 90
Internet Public Library: 29
Learn2: 276
Library of Congress: 227
LookSmart: 13
Mining Company (sites): 170
Research It (Itools): 132
Science Surf: 95
Virtual Reference Desk: 83

INDEX (BY SITE NUMBER)

Search Engines
AltaVista: 180
Ancestors: 208
Area Code: 49
Ask Jeeves: 284
Beaucoup: 32
Country Search: 174
Cultural Events: 231
E-mail Search: 269
Excite: 7, 299
FedEx: 210
Internet Sleuth: 266
Lycos: 7
Medical: 27
Parks: 135
Patents: 152
Phone Numbers: 73
Profusion: 140
Search.com (C/Net): 267
SIC Codes: 280
UPS: 210
Yahoo!: 260, 299
Zip Codes: 277

Shopping
Gifts Online: 165

Sports
Arena Layouts: 97
Baseball Statistics: 120
College: 236
ESPN: 69

Sports (cont.)
Fastball: 240
Golf: 178, 232
Major League Baseball: 240
NBA: 104
NFL: 54
NHL: 264
Sports Network: 291
Total Baseball: 120

Stocks/Investments
Dow Jones Average: 203
Earning Reports: 218
Financial Network: 173
IPOs: 199
Microsoft Investor: 6
Motley Fool: 77
Mutual Funds: 37, 164
News Alert: 220
Play the Market: 119
Purchase One Share: 43
Purchase Stocks: 192
Stock Markets: 282
Stockfind: 167
Stocksmart: 221
Yahoo Quotes: 6
Young Investor: 126

Travel
Airlines: 238
Business Traveler: 144
Currency Converter: 61

Travel (cont.)
City Guides: 15, 102, 147, 196
City Locations: 111
Expedia: 107
FAA: 161
Fodor's: 293
Frommer's: 293
Hotels: 237
New York City: 215
Road Construction: 226
Travel Language: 53
Travel Source: 293
Travelocity: 84
Trip (Directions): 118
Trip.com: 12
Yahoo Flights: 274
Zip2 Directions: 108

Weather
Current Weather: 265
Historical Weather: 41
Weather Channel: 265

The Incredible Newsletter

If you are enjoying this book, you can also arrange to receive a steady stream of more "incredible Internet things," delivered directly to your e-mail address.

The Leebow Letter, Ken Leebow's weekly e-mail newsletter, provides new sites, updates on existing ones and information about other happenings on the Internet.

For more details about *The Leebow Letter* and how to subscribe, send an e-mail to:

Newsletter@Mindspring.com

Books by Ken Leebow

300 Incredible Things to Do on the Internet

300 Incredible Things for Kids on the Internet

300 Incredible Sports Sites on the Internet